RENT RECEIPT BOOK

Receipt

Name	Date

DESCRIPTION OF ITEMS/SERVICE PURCHASED	AMOUNT
TOTAL	

RECEIVED BY ______________________ APPROVED BY ______________________

Receipt

Name	Date

DESCRIPTION OF ITEMS/SERVICE PURCHASED	AMOUNT
TOTAL	

RECEIVED BY ______________________ APPROVED BY ______________________

Receipt

Name	Date

DESCRIPTION OF ITEMS/SERVICE PURCHASED	AMOUNT
TOTAL	

RECEIVED BY ______________________ APPROVED BY ______________________

Receipt

Name	Date

DESCRIPTION OF ITEMS/SERVICE PURCHASED	AMOUNT
TOTAL	

RECEIVED BY ______________________ APPROVED BY ______________________

Receipt

Name	Date

DESCRIPTION OF ITEMS/SERVICE PURCHASED	AMOUNT
TOTAL	

RECEIVED BY ______________________ APPROVED BY ______________________

Receipt

Name	Date

DESCRIPTION OF ITEMS/SERVICE PURCHASED	AMOUNT
TOTAL	

RECEIVED BY ______________________ APPROVED BY ______________________

Receipt

Name	Date

DESCRIPTION OF ITEMS/SERVICE PURCHASED	AMOUNT
TOTAL	

RECEIVED BY ______________________ APPROVED BY ______________________

Receipt

Name	Date

DESCRIPTION OF ITEMS/SERVICE PURCHASED	AMOUNT
TOTAL	

RECEIVED BY ______________________ APPROVED BY ______________________

Receipt

Name	**Date**

DESCRIPTION OF ITEMS/SERVICE PURCHASED	AMOUNT
TOTAL	

RECEIVED BY ______________________ APPROVED BY ______________________

Receipt

Name	**Date**

DESCRIPTION OF ITEMS/SERVICE PURCHASED	AMOUNT
TOTAL	

RECEIVED BY ______________________ APPROVED BY ______________________

Receipt

Name	Date

DESCRIPTION OF ITEMS/SERVICE PURCHASED	AMOUNT
TOTAL	

RECEIVED BY ____________________ APPROVED BY ____________________

Receipt

Name	Date

DESCRIPTION OF ITEMS/SERVICE PURCHASED	AMOUNT
TOTAL	

RECEIVED BY ____________________ APPROVED BY ____________________

Receipt

Name	Date

DESCRIPTION OF ITEMS/SERVICE PURCHASED	AMOUNT
TOTAL	

RECEIVED BY ______________________ APPROVED BY ______________________

Receipt

Name	Date

DESCRIPTION OF ITEMS/SERVICE PURCHASED	AMOUNT
TOTAL	

RECEIVED BY ______________________ APPROVED BY ______________________

Receipt

Name	Date

DESCRIPTION OF ITEMS/SERVICE PURCHASED	AMOUNT
TOTAL	

RECEIVED BY ______________________ APPROVED BY ______________________

Receipt

Name	Date

DESCRIPTION OF ITEMS/SERVICE PURCHASED	AMOUNT
TOTAL	

RECEIVED BY ______________________ APPROVED BY ______________________

Receipt

Name	Date

DESCRIPTION OF ITEMS/SERVICE PURCHASED	AMOUNT
TOTAL	

RECEIVED BY ______________________ APPROVED BY ______________________

Receipt

Name	Date

DESCRIPTION OF ITEMS/SERVICE PURCHASED	AMOUNT
TOTAL	

RECEIVED BY ______________________ APPROVED BY ______________________

Receipt

Name	Date

DESCRIPTION OF ITEMS/SERVICE PURCHASED	AMOUNT
TOTAL	

RECEIVED BY ______________________ APPROVED BY ______________________

Receipt

Name	Date

DESCRIPTION OF ITEMS/SERVICE PURCHASED	AMOUNT
TOTAL	

RECEIVED BY ______________________ APPROVED BY ______________________

Receipt

Name	Date

DESCRIPTION OF ITEMS/SERVICE PURCHASED	AMOUNT
TOTAL	

RECEIVED BY ______________________ APPROVED BY ______________________

Receipt

Name	Date

DESCRIPTION OF ITEMS/SERVICE PURCHASED	AMOUNT
TOTAL	

RECEIVED BY ______________________ APPROVED BY ______________________

Receipt

Name	Date

DESCRIPTION OF ITEMS/SERVICE PURCHASED	AMOUNT
TOTAL	

RECEIVED BY ______________________ APPROVED BY ______________________

Receipt

Name	Date

DESCRIPTION OF ITEMS/SERVICE PURCHASED	AMOUNT
TOTAL	

RECEIVED BY ______________________ APPROVED BY ______________________

Receipt

Name	Date

DESCRIPTION OF ITEMS/SERVICE PURCHASED	AMOUNT
TOTAL	

RECEIVED BY ______________________ APPROVED BY ______________________

Receipt

Name	Date

DESCRIPTION OF ITEMS/SERVICE PURCHASED	AMOUNT
TOTAL	

RECEIVED BY ______________________ APPROVED BY ______________________

Receipt

Name	Date

DESCRIPTION OF ITEMS/SERVICE PURCHASED	AMOUNT
TOTAL	

RECEIVED BY ______________________ APPROVED BY ______________________

Receipt

Name	Date

DESCRIPTION OF ITEMS/SERVICE PURCHASED	AMOUNT
TOTAL	

RECEIVED BY ______________________ APPROVED BY ______________________

Receipt

Name	Date

DESCRIPTION OF ITEMS/SERVICE PURCHASED	AMOUNT
TOTAL	

RECEIVED BY ______________________ APPROVED BY ______________________

Receipt

Name	Date

DESCRIPTION OF ITEMS/SERVICE PURCHASED	AMOUNT
TOTAL	

RECEIVED BY ______________________ APPROVED BY ______________________

Receipt

Name	Date

DESCRIPTION OF ITEMS/SERVICE PURCHASED	AMOUNT
TOTAL	

RECEIVED BY ____________________ APPROVED BY ____________________

Receipt

Name	Date

DESCRIPTION OF ITEMS/SERVICE PURCHASED	AMOUNT
TOTAL	

RECEIVED BY ____________________ APPROVED BY ____________________

Receipt

Name	Date

DESCRIPTION OF ITEMS/SERVICE PURCHASED	AMOUNT
TOTAL	

RECEIVED BY ______________________ APPROVED BY ______________________

Receipt

Name	Date

DESCRIPTION OF ITEMS/SERVICE PURCHASED	AMOUNT
TOTAL	

RECEIVED BY ______________________ APPROVED BY ______________________

Receipt

Name	Date

DESCRIPTION OF ITEMS/SERVICE PURCHASED	AMOUNT
TOTAL	

RECEIVED BY ____________________ APPROVED BY ____________________

Receipt

Name	Date

DESCRIPTION OF ITEMS/SERVICE PURCHASED	AMOUNT
TOTAL	

RECEIVED BY ____________________ APPROVED BY ____________________

Receipt

Name	Date

DESCRIPTION OF ITEMS/SERVICE PURCHASED	AMOUNT
TOTAL	

RECEIVED BY ______________________ APPROVED BY ______________________

Receipt

Name	Date

DESCRIPTION OF ITEMS/SERVICE PURCHASED	AMOUNT
TOTAL	

RECEIVED BY ______________________ APPROVED BY ______________________

Receipt

Name	Date

DESCRIPTION OF ITEMS/SERVICE PURCHASED	AMOUNT
TOTAL	

RECEIVED BY ____________________ APPROVED BY ____________________

Receipt

Name	Date

DESCRIPTION OF ITEMS/SERVICE PURCHASED	AMOUNT
TOTAL	

RECEIVED BY ____________________ APPROVED BY ____________________

Receipt

Name	Date

DESCRIPTION OF ITEMS/SERVICE PURCHASED	AMOUNT
TOTAL	

RECEIVED BY ____________________ APPROVED BY ____________________

Receipt

Name	Date

DESCRIPTION OF ITEMS/SERVICE PURCHASED	AMOUNT
TOTAL	

RECEIVED BY ____________________ APPROVED BY ____________________

Receipt

Name	Date

DESCRIPTION OF ITEMS/SERVICE PURCHASED	AMOUNT
TOTAL	

RECEIVED BY ______________________ APPROVED BY ______________________

Receipt

Name	Date

DESCRIPTION OF ITEMS/SERVICE PURCHASED	AMOUNT
TOTAL	

RECEIVED BY ______________________ APPROVED BY ______________________

Receipt

Name	Date

DESCRIPTION OF ITEMS/SERVICE PURCHASED	AMOUNT
TOTAL	

RECEIVED BY ______________________ APPROVED BY ______________________

Receipt

Name	Date

DESCRIPTION OF ITEMS/SERVICE PURCHASED	AMOUNT
TOTAL	

RECEIVED BY ______________________ APPROVED BY ______________________

Receipt

Name	Date

DESCRIPTION OF ITEMS/SERVICE PURCHASED	AMOUNT
TOTAL	

RECEIVED BY ______________________ APPROVED BY ______________________

Receipt

Name	Date

DESCRIPTION OF ITEMS/SERVICE PURCHASED	AMOUNT
TOTAL	

RECEIVED BY ______________________ APPROVED BY ______________________

Receipt

Name	Date

DESCRIPTION OF ITEMS/SERVICE PURCHASED	AMOUNT
TOTAL	

RECEIVED BY ______________________ APPROVED BY ______________________

Receipt

Name	Date

DESCRIPTION OF ITEMS/SERVICE PURCHASED	AMOUNT
TOTAL	

RECEIVED BY ______________________ APPROVED BY ______________________

Receipt

Name	Date

DESCRIPTION OF ITEMS/SERVICE PURCHASED	AMOUNT
TOTAL	

RECEIVED BY ______________________ APPROVED BY ______________________

Receipt

Name	Date

DESCRIPTION OF ITEMS/SERVICE PURCHASED	AMOUNT
TOTAL	

RECEIVED BY ______________________ APPROVED BY ______________________

Receipt

Name	Date

DESCRIPTION OF ITEMS/SERVICE PURCHASED	AMOUNT
TOTAL	

RECEIVED BY ______________________ APPROVED BY ______________________

Receipt

Name	Date

DESCRIPTION OF ITEMS/SERVICE PURCHASED	AMOUNT
TOTAL	

RECEIVED BY ______________________ APPROVED BY ______________________

Receipt

Name	Date

DESCRIPTION OF ITEMS/SERVICE PURCHASED	AMOUNT
TOTAL	

RECEIVED BY ____________________ APPROVED BY ____________________

Receipt

Name	Date

DESCRIPTION OF ITEMS/SERVICE PURCHASED	AMOUNT
TOTAL	

RECEIVED BY ____________________ APPROVED BY ____________________

Receipt

Name	Date

DESCRIPTION OF ITEMS/SERVICE PURCHASED	AMOUNT
TOTAL	

RECEIVED BY ______________________ APPROVED BY ______________________

Receipt

Name	Date

DESCRIPTION OF ITEMS/SERVICE PURCHASED	AMOUNT
TOTAL	

RECEIVED BY ______________________ APPROVED BY ______________________

Receipt

Name	Date

DESCRIPTION OF ITEMS/SERVICE PURCHASED	AMOUNT
TOTAL	

RECEIVED BY ______________________ APPROVED BY ______________________

Receipt

Name	Date

DESCRIPTION OF ITEMS/SERVICE PURCHASED	AMOUNT
TOTAL	

RECEIVED BY ______________________ APPROVED BY ______________________

Receipt

Name	Date

DESCRIPTION OF ITEMS/SERVICE PURCHASED	AMOUNT
TOTAL	

RECEIVED BY ______________________ APPROVED BY ______________________

Receipt

Name	Date

DESCRIPTION OF ITEMS/SERVICE PURCHASED	AMOUNT
TOTAL	

RECEIVED BY ______________________ APPROVED BY ______________________

Receipt

Name	Date

DESCRIPTION OF ITEMS/SERVICE PURCHASED	AMOUNT
TOTAL	

RECEIVED BY ____________________ APPROVED BY ____________________

Receipt

Name	Date

DESCRIPTION OF ITEMS/SERVICE PURCHASED	AMOUNT
TOTAL	

RECEIVED BY ____________________ APPROVED BY ____________________

Receipt

Name	Date

DESCRIPTION OF ITEMS/SERVICE PURCHASED	AMOUNT
TOTAL	

RECEIVED BY ______________________ APPROVED BY ______________________

Receipt

Name	Date

DESCRIPTION OF ITEMS/SERVICE PURCHASED	AMOUNT
TOTAL	

RECEIVED BY ______________________ APPROVED BY ______________________

Receipt

Name	Date

DESCRIPTION OF ITEMS/SERVICE PURCHASED	AMOUNT
TOTAL	

RECEIVED BY ______________________ APPROVED BY ______________________

Receipt

Name	Date

DESCRIPTION OF ITEMS/SERVICE PURCHASED	AMOUNT
TOTAL	

RECEIVED BY ______________________ APPROVED BY ______________________

Receipt

Name	Date

DESCRIPTION OF ITEMS/SERVICE PURCHASED	AMOUNT
TOTAL	

RECEIVED BY ____________________ APPROVED BY ____________________

Receipt

Name	Date

DESCRIPTION OF ITEMS/SERVICE PURCHASED	AMOUNT
TOTAL	

RECEIVED BY ____________________ APPROVED BY ____________________

Receipt

Name	Date

DESCRIPTION OF ITEMS/SERVICE PURCHASED	AMOUNT
TOTAL	

RECEIVED BY ______________________ APPROVED BY ______________________

Receipt

Name	Date

DESCRIPTION OF ITEMS/SERVICE PURCHASED	AMOUNT
TOTAL	

RECEIVED BY ______________________ APPROVED BY ______________________

Receipt

Name	Date

DESCRIPTION OF ITEMS/SERVICE PURCHASED	AMOUNT
TOTAL	

RECEIVED BY ____________________ APPROVED BY ____________________

Receipt

Name	Date

DESCRIPTION OF ITEMS/SERVICE PURCHASED	AMOUNT
TOTAL	

RECEIVED BY ____________________ APPROVED BY ____________________

Receipt

Name	Date

DESCRIPTION OF ITEMS/SERVICE PURCHASED	AMOUNT
TOTAL	

RECEIVED BY ____________________ APPROVED BY ____________________

Receipt

Name	Date

DESCRIPTION OF ITEMS/SERVICE PURCHASED	AMOUNT
TOTAL	

RECEIVED BY ____________________ APPROVED BY ____________________

Receipt

Name	Date

DESCRIPTION OF ITEMS/SERVICE PURCHASED	AMOUNT
TOTAL	

RECEIVED BY ______________________ APPROVED BY ______________________

Receipt

Name	Date

DESCRIPTION OF ITEMS/SERVICE PURCHASED	AMOUNT
TOTAL	

RECEIVED BY ______________________ APPROVED BY ______________________

Receipt

Name	Date

DESCRIPTION OF ITEMS/SERVICE PURCHASED	AMOUNT
TOTAL	

RECEIVED BY ____________________ APPROVED BY ____________________

Receipt

Name	Date

DESCRIPTION OF ITEMS/SERVICE PURCHASED	AMOUNT
TOTAL	

RECEIVED BY ____________________ APPROVED BY ____________________

Receipt

Name	Date

DESCRIPTION OF ITEMS/SERVICE PURCHASED	AMOUNT
TOTAL	

RECEIVED BY ______________________ APPROVED BY ______________________

Receipt

Name	Date

DESCRIPTION OF ITEMS/SERVICE PURCHASED	AMOUNT
TOTAL	

RECEIVED BY ______________________ APPROVED BY ______________________

Receipt

Name	Date

DESCRIPTION OF ITEMS/SERVICE PURCHASED	AMOUNT
TOTAL	

RECEIVED BY ____________________ APPROVED BY ____________________

Receipt

Name	Date

DESCRIPTION OF ITEMS/SERVICE PURCHASED	AMOUNT
TOTAL	

RECEIVED BY ____________________ APPROVED BY ____________________

Receipt

Name	Date

DESCRIPTION OF ITEMS/SERVICE PURCHASED	AMOUNT
TOTAL	

RECEIVED BY ______________________ APPROVED BY ______________________

Receipt

Name	Date

DESCRIPTION OF ITEMS/SERVICE PURCHASED	AMOUNT
TOTAL	

RECEIVED BY ______________________ APPROVED BY ______________________

Receipt

Name	Date

DESCRIPTION OF ITEMS/SERVICE PURCHASED	AMOUNT
TOTAL	

RECEIVED BY ______________________ APPROVED BY ______________________

Receipt

Name	Date

DESCRIPTION OF ITEMS/SERVICE PURCHASED	AMOUNT
TOTAL	

RECEIVED BY ______________________ APPROVED BY ______________________

Receipt

Name	Date

DESCRIPTION OF ITEMS/SERVICE PURCHASED	AMOUNT
TOTAL	

RECEIVED BY ______________________ APPROVED BY ______________________

Receipt

Name	Date

DESCRIPTION OF ITEMS/SERVICE PURCHASED	AMOUNT
TOTAL	

RECEIVED BY ______________________ APPROVED BY ______________________

Receipt

Name	Date

DESCRIPTION OF ITEMS/SERVICE PURCHASED	AMOUNT
TOTAL	

RECEIVED BY ____________________ APPROVED BY ____________________

Receipt

Name	Date

DESCRIPTION OF ITEMS/SERVICE PURCHASED	AMOUNT
TOTAL	

RECEIVED BY ____________________ APPROVED BY ____________________

Receipt

Name	Date

DESCRIPTION OF ITEMS/SERVICE PURCHASED	AMOUNT
TOTAL	

RECEIVED BY ____________________ APPROVED BY ____________________

Receipt

Name	Date

DESCRIPTION OF ITEMS/SERVICE PURCHASED	AMOUNT
TOTAL	

RECEIVED BY ____________________ APPROVED BY ____________________

Receipt

Name	Date

DESCRIPTION OF ITEMS/SERVICE PURCHASED	AMOUNT
TOTAL	

RECEIVED BY ____________________ APPROVED BY ____________________

Receipt

Name	Date

DESCRIPTION OF ITEMS/SERVICE PURCHASED	AMOUNT
TOTAL	

RECEIVED BY ____________________ APPROVED BY ____________________

www.ingramcontent.com/pod-product-compliance
Lightning Source LLC
LaVergne TN
LVHW080000210926
848481LV00012B/3637
* 9 7 9 8 8 6 9 4 5 5 2 5 3 *